MIGHTY MUSCLE CARS

CHEVROLET CORVETTE

Megan Borgert-Spaniol

Big Buddy Books

An Imprint of Abdo Publishing
abdobooks.com

abdobooks.com

Published by Abdo Publishing, a division of ABDO, PO Box 398166, Minneapolis, Minnesota 55439. Copyright © 2021 by Abdo Consulting Group, Inc. International copyrights reserved in all countries. No part of this book may be reproduced in any form without written permission from the publisher. Big Buddy Books™ is a trademark and logo of Abdo Publishing.

Printed in the United States of America, North Mankato, Minnesota
082020
012021

Design: Christa Schneider, Mighty Media, Inc.
Production: Mighty Media, Inc.
Editor: Liz Salzmann

Cover Photograph: Shutterstock Images

Interior Photographs: Michael Barera/Wikimedia Commons, pp. 8, 9; Shutterstock Images, pp. 4, 5, 7, 10, 11, 14, 15, 16, 17, 18, 19, 20, 21, 22, 23, 24, 25, 26, 27, 28, 29; Sicnag/Flickr, p. 28 (1953); sv1ambo/Flickr, pp. 12, 13; sv1ambo/Wikimedia Commons, p. 28 (1963)

Design Elements: Shutterstock Images

Library of Congress Control Number: 2020931626

Publisher's Cataloging-in-Publication Data
Names: Borgert-Spaniol, Megan, author.
Title: Chevrolet Corvette / by Megan Borgert-Spaniol
Description: Minneapolis, Minnesota : Abdo Publishing, 2021 | Series: Mighty muscle cars | Includes online resources and index
Identifiers: ISBN 9781532193248 (lib. bdg.) | ISBN 9781098211882 (ebook)
Subjects: LCSH: Muscle cars--Juvenile literature. | Motor vehicles--Juvenile literature. | Automobiles--Customizing--Juvenile literature. | Hot rods--Juvenile literature.
Classification: DDC 629.222--dc23

CONTENTS

KING CORVETTE

A 2017 Chevrolet Corvette growls at the starting line. To its left, the engine of a Ford Mustang rumbles. The drivers wait for the green lights. Then they're off!

The Corvette takes an early lead. Then it falls behind the Mustang. In the final seconds of the drag race, the Corvette pulls ahead. It wins with a time of 11 seconds!

DID YOU KNOW?

In a drag race, two cars race on a straight track called a drag strip. Most drag strips are one-eighth mile (0.2 km) or one-quarter mile (0.4 km) long.

AMERICAN MUSCLE

The Chevrolet Corvette is one of the most iconic muscle cars on the market. Muscle cars are American high-performance cars. They are built for power and speed.

The first muscle car came out in 1949. Muscle cars soon became widely popular in the 1960s. They were made for drag racing. But most could also be driven on city streets.

CHEVROLET CORVETTE
FAST FACTS

Manufacturer: Chevrolet, a division of
General Motors (GM)

First model year: 1953

Top speed: 212 miles per hour (341 km/h)

Top horsepower: 755 hp

Top acceleration: 0 to 60 miles per hour
(96 km/h) in 2.85 seconds

CHEVROLET CLASSIC

The Chevrolet Corvette got its start in Detroit, Michigan. Chevrolet Motor Company formed there in 1911. The company was named after cofounder Louis Chevrolet. He was a Swiss race car driver. Chevrolet Motor Company later became part of General Motors (GM). The company grew steadily. In 1934, Chevrolet built its ten millionth car!

Chevrolet's first model was known as the "Classic Six."

WARS AND WARSHIPS

During **World War II**, Chevrolet stopped making cars. Instead, it made supplies for the US military. The war ended in 1945. Chevrolet started making cars again.

In 1953, Chevrolet presented a two-seater sports car at a New York car show. The car was named *Corvette* after a type of small warship. This first Corvette was a **concept car**. But buyers were interested! So that year, Chevrolet built 300 of them.

The 300 Corvettes produced in 1953 were all white with red interiors.

1953

1953 CHEVROLET CORVETTE

The first time the public saw Harley Earl's "dream car," the Corvette (code named Project Opel), was in January 1953 at the Motorama [...] the Corvette went into full production at a GM facility in [...] [...]higan. On June 30, 1953,

This is the Corvette that started it all — Chevrolet's first true sports car. The 1953 Corvette featured an *innovative fiberglass body* that made for a much lighter car, more easily molded into complex shapes than traditional steel-constru[...] [...]here were only 300 Corvettes produced in 1953 [...]atures of [...]rvette

1955 BEL AIR SPO[...]

Occasionally, a new car arriv[...] standout is the 1955 Bel Air [...] to its cultural roots, the longe[...] state-of-the-art features.

A *new 265-cubic-inch "Turb[...]* block engine family — was op[...] aluminum pistons, lightweigh[...] dimensions were among the [...] the most successful engine i[...]

STING RAY

The second-**generation** Corvette came in 1963. That year brought the Corvette Sting Ray. This model came in both a **convertible** and **coupe** style.

The Sting Ray was smaller than the first generation. It was narrower at the rear. This gave it a sleek look. The 1963 model also had a split rear window.

DID YOU KNOW?

In the 1960s, Chevrolet offered all US astronauts a deal. They could use a car for a year for just one dollar. Most astronauts chose to drive Corvettes!

The split rear window only lasted one model year. Many people didn't like it.

SLICING THROUGH AIR

The next 20 years brought bold new **designs** for the Corvette. In 1968, the third **generation**, or C3, came out. This model was long and low to the ground. It had a flat rear end and a **spoiler**.

Production of the C4 Corvette began in 1983. The C4 had the lowest drag yet. A car with low drag cuts easily through the air.

DID YOU KNOW?

In 1978, the C3 Corvette was used as a pace car for the Indianapolis 500.

The C4 featured a one-piece roof that could be removed for open-air driving.

COMPLETE REDESIGN

Chevrolet was not done improving the Corvette. In 1997, it released the C5. This Corvette featured a new engine, lighter body, and better steering control. Drivers considered it the first model with equal parts comfort and performance.

The C6 Corvette came out in 2005. It had a similar look to the C5. But the C6's engine was more powerful. It also offered the Corvette's first **navigation system**.

A 1969 C2 (*left*) and 1999 C5 (*right*) show how the Corvette changed over 30 years.

RETURN OF THE RAY

The C7 Corvette brought back the Sting Ray name with a new twist. The 2014 Corvette Stingray had more than 450 horsepower (hp). It could hit 60 miles per hour (96 km/h) in less than four seconds. However, a more powerful model wasn't far off!

DID YOU KNOW?

Horsepower (hp) is a measure of how powerful an engine is. One hp equals the power needed to lift a 550-pound (249 kg) weight up one foot (0.3 m) in one second.

The C7 Corvette debuted a new version of its crossed-flags logo and hood badge.

UNDER THE HOOD

755 hp
V8 engine

CHEVROLET CORVETTE ZR1

In 2019, Chevrolet built the fastest, most powerful Corvette yet. The ZR1 had a 755 hp engine. The car could reach 60 miles per hour (96 km/h) in 2.85 seconds. It also had a top track speed of 212 miles per hour (341 km/h)!

Manual or automatic transmission

Two doors

Rear-wheel drive

19-inch front and 20-inch rear wheels

CAR ENGINES 101

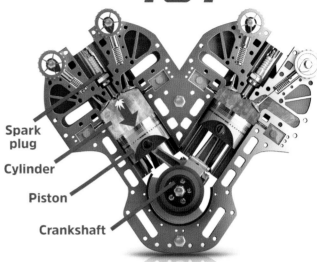

Spark plug

Cylinder

Piston

Crankshaft

Car engines turn the energy in gasoline into motion. Fuel and air are pumped into the engine's **cylinders**. A spark creates an explosion. The explosion pushes the **piston** down to turn the **crankshaft**. This is a bit like a foot pushing down on a bicycle pedal. At high speed, these explosions happen thousands of times a minute!

TEAM CORVETTE

The Corvette was known for racing. In 1960, American driver Briggs Cunningham **debuted** the Corvette at Le Mans. This is a 24-hour race in France. The Corvette finished first in its class!

In 1999, Corvette created an official racing team. It is named Corvette Racing. Since 2001, the team has won eight times at Le Mans. That year, the team also won at another 24-hour race called the Rolex 24 at Daytona.

A C6 Corvette makes a pit stop at the 2008 Le Mans race. Pit stops are for refueling, changing tires, and making repairs.

POP CULTURE CORVETTES

The Corvette has also found fame in **pop culture**. The 1960s TV show *Route 66* featured a 1963 Corvette Sting Ray. This show made the car a **symbol** of freedom and adventure. In 1982, music icon Prince released the hit song "Little Red Corvette."

Actor Johnny Depp drove a C1 Corvette in the 2011 movie *The Rum Diary*. And in 2012, a C7 Corvette was added to the popular racing video game *Gran Turismo 5*.

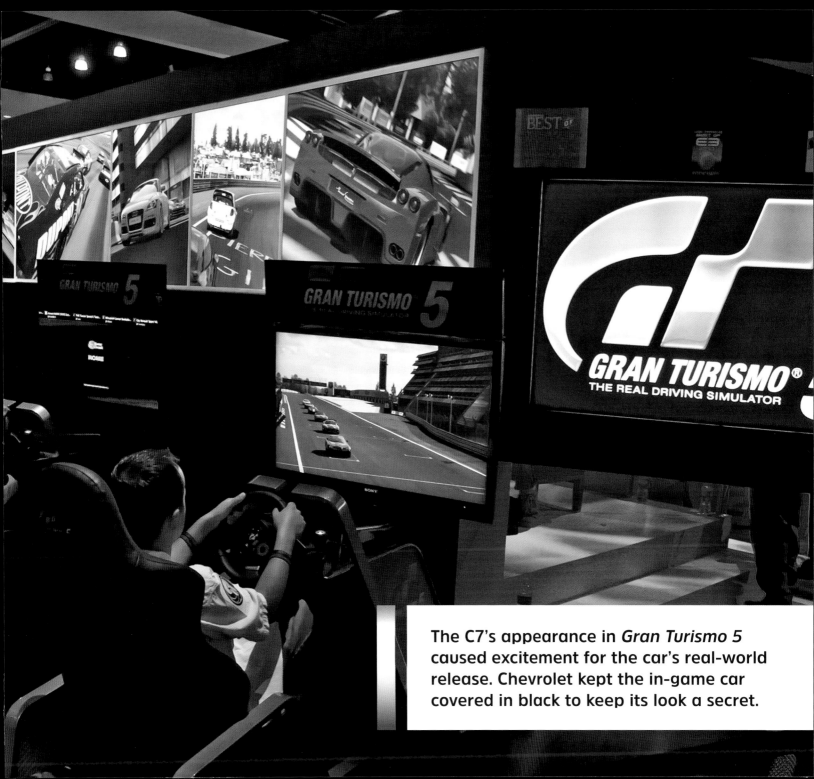

The C7's appearance in *Gran Turismo 5* caused excitement for the car's real-world release. Chevrolet kept the in-game car covered in black to keep its look a secret.

ALL-NEW THRILLS

Chevrolet raced into a new decade with the 2020 Corvette Stingray. The new car treated drivers to improved performance. Its 495-horsepower engine allowed a top speed of 194 miles per hour (312 km/h)! Nearly 70 years after its **debut**, the Corvette continues to be a thrilling ride.

The 2020 Stingray is the first Corvette with two fuel tanks. The tanks are placed near each rear wheel.

Chevrolet Motor Company was born in Detroit, Michigan.

The Corvette Sting Ray **debuted** with a sleek new look.

Chevrolet presented a major **redesign** of the Corvette, including a new engine.

1911

1963

1997

1953

1968

Chevrolet presented the first Corvette at a New York car show.

The C3 Corvette came out with a **spoiler**.

The C6 Corvette **debuted** with a more powerful engine than the C5.

Chevrolet started a new decade with the 2020 Corvette Stingray.

2005

2020

1999

2014

2019

Corvette Racing was established as the official Corvette racing team.

The new Corvette Stingray model boasted more than 450 horsepower.

Chevrolet unveiled the ZR1, the fastest, most powerful Corvette model yet.

concept car—a car produced as a model to show a new style or technology but not made available for sale.

convertible—a car with a roof that can be lowered or removed.

coupe—a car with a fixed roof, two doors, and two or four seats.

crankshaft—a long, metal rod that transfers energy from the engine through the transmission and eventually to the wheels.

cylinder—a shaft in which a piston of an engine moves.

debut—a first appearance. To debut is to appear for the first time or present something for the first time.

design (dih-ZINE)—a plan for how something will appear or work. To redesign is to make changes to the way an existing thing appears or works.

generation—a class of objects created from an earlier type.

navigation system—an electronic device that shows how to get from one place to another.

pace car—a car that leads competing race cars during warm-up laps. A pace car also enters the track during a race to slow the pace if there are hazardous conditions.

piston—a part in an engine that moves up and down inside the cylinder.

pop culture—short for *popular culture*. People, things, and events that are commonly well-known throughout a society. Pop culture includes products, movies, TV shows, music, celebrities, sports, and more.

spoiler—a part at the rear of a car that prevents the air flowing over the car from slipping under the car and lifting it up.

symbol (SIHM-buhl)—an object or mark that stands for an idea.

World War II—a war fought in Europe, Asia, and Africa from 1939 to 1945.

ONLINE RESOURCES

Booklinks
NONFICTION NETWORK
FREE! ONLINE NONFICTION RESOURCES

To learn more about the Chevrolet Corvette, please visit **abdobooklinks.com** or scan this QR code. These links are routinely monitored and updated to provide the most current information available.

INDEX